This book belongs to
_____

Front: Leopoldskron Palace
Back: Mirabell Garden

First edition 2006
Print: Pfeifer Druck & Media, Haugsdorf

© 2006 – All rights reserved

ISBN Nr. 978-3-9502181-1-4

The work is protected by copyright laws. No part of this work, its text or illustrations may be reproduced without the written permission of the publisher. The same restrictions apply to the production of facsimiles and translations as well as microfilming and electronic data processing.

The Singing Family of Salzburg

A story by Margret Springl

Illustrated by Regine Otrel

The most important thing in life is:
To find out the will of god
and then do it.

Maria von Trapp

Origin: Testament Franz Wasner (post- and signaturecard)

For my daughter Rebecca

Old Town of Salzburg

The singing family of Salzburg

Once upon a time there was a young woman named Maria who lived in a little house on a hill surrounded by shady maple trees. She gave music and singing lessons to the sisters at a nearby abbey and enjoyed a great deal of pleasure from her work. Every evening at sunset, the bells from the cathedral rang out signaling the end of the day. Those evenings, Maria made herself comfortable on a bench under a tree, playing on her guitar and singing a beautiful song.

At this time as well, a noble family in town was experiencing a great deal of suffering. The family's mother had died after a long illness and left her husband behind with seven children. Hearing this, the young woman packed her suitcase and went to the house of the family where she received employment for arranging the household and providing the children with useful instructions.

Frohnburg Palace

Imberg Street

The Mirabell Stairs

With her friendly and jovial nature, she easily captured the hearts of the members of the family. Therefore, it was not surprising when the father of the family soon asked her to marry him and to stay with him and the children forever. Cheerfully, the young woman agreed and they spent a wonderful time together with their children.

Hellbrunn Palace

*I*n the evening, they played their instruments and sang together or practiced new songs. Their lovely voices gave the music a magical sound. In time, the number of compositions grew along with the number of children in the house.

They all helped and supported each other. They seldom quarreled and rarely exchanged angry words. But when they did, they apologized to each other and reconciled with one another, promising to change for the better.

One evening, a man knocked at the door of the family's house and asked if it would be possible to stay there for the night because it was quite late and he was very tired. Since the house was large and many rooms were empty, the family agreed and he was also invited to listen to their evening singing practice.

They found out that the visitor was a profound lover of music himself. He knew a lot about songs and compositions and conducted all evening long.

guitar

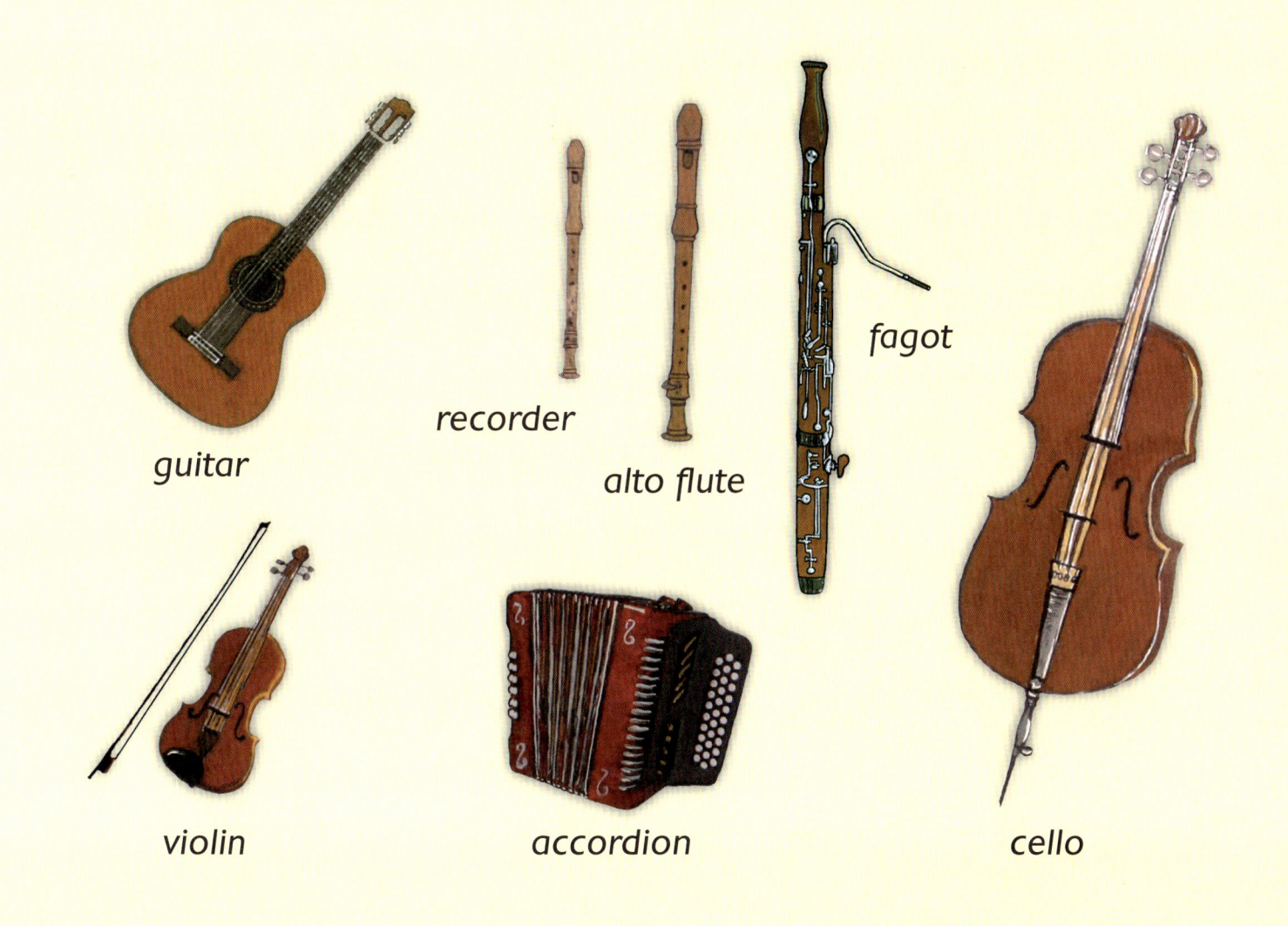

recorder

alto flute

fagot

violin

accordion

cello

Soon, the visitor came back again to stay, bringing his friends and relatives with him. He became a close friend of the family and after a while, the family was able to afford new musical instruments with the money they received from letting their spare rooms.

The family's passion and love for music and their songs were so strong that more and more people around them delighted in hearing the family sing and play. One day, the family was asked to join an annual song competition. They practiced faithfully and worked hard until the big day finally arrived. The family anxiously took their places on stage, awaiting the sign from the concertmaster. Their voices soared majestically as they sang their most beautiful pieces.

Felsenreitschule in the festival theater

The audience cheered enthusiastically and the family sang again at the top of their voices. During the thunderous applause, the jury proudly presented the family with the first prize. From that moment on, they made regular appearances at different events and soon began giving concerts to the public.

Horsepond

$\mathcal{T}$hings could have remained just as wonderful as they were if it hadn't been for influential people with bad intentions and important functions. And so it happened that one day, a war broke out. Deadly weapons were produced, food became scarce and the citizens lived in fear and terror.

This was very painful for the family who had experienced nothing but love and peace until this time. In a family council, they decided not to agree to this sort of violence and instead, to flee to the United States of America. Soon, with their most important belongings they sailed across the ocean to the foreign land.

New York – USA

Many new and different things had to be learned in this country. A different language, different people, a different culture, different clothes, even the food was completely different from that which the family was used to.

Still, they did not become discouraged and, thanks to the country's dear and helpful inhabitants, they soon grew accustomed to their new home. Due to their friendly and positive dispositions, they easily made new friends.

In the meantime, they continued to sing songs, new and old. In order to transport their musical instruments, they bought an old bus and drove from town to town to sing for people.

*E*veryone who met them during their travels was astounded by their appearance. The bus full of musical instruments completed the family's image.

Soon, they became famous for the wonderful songs they sang. People traveled from far and wide to see the family singing on stage. The concert halls they played in were usually left with standing room only.

Boston

Vermont

One day, as they were returning home from a concert, they crossed a valley with sun-drenched hills and lush green meadows. A crystal clear mountain stream ran through the valley. The birds were singing and the snow-capped mountains glistened in the sunlight. This place reminded them of Salzburg so much that they decided to settle there.

𝒯hey bought an old farmhouse in the midst of this beautiful landscape and, together, they renovated it with a great deal of skill and effort, soon restoring it to its old glory.

They bought cows, horses, sheep and chickens and spent their spare time working together on the farm whenever they were not traveling for concerts. The family, which had only lived in hotels, guesthouses or in their friends' homes so far was very proud of their new home and expressed their emotions through working and singing.

However, the family did not sing merely to enrich themselves and acquire possessions. Some of their earnings were also set aside for charitable causes. For example, they helped when the roof of the school got damaged and needed to be repaired. They also sent relief parcels to poor people back in their home town in Europe. Everyone in the family found it important to help their neighbors and to fill the hearts of people with the joy their music brought.

Through their constant performances, the family soon became well-known even beyond their own country's borders. Their songs brought people happiness and their singing drove away feelings such as fear and envy, replacing them with kindness and brotherly love. The family was aware of these precious moments. In order to make them last, they decided to establish a meeting place for people who loved to sing. In the process, they founded a musical society.

They received permission to use an old storage building for this purpose and transformed it into a singing camp. There, they regularly met with interested persons in order to play music and share ideas.

The family received letters and postcards daily from all over the world. To show their gratitude, they traveled to far-away continents and small islands across the globe. They visited people, talked with them about their culture, laughed with them and sang songs together.

To their great satisfaction, the family realized that their singing and music had helped them succeed in passing joy onto others. In this way, they had contributed to keep peace on earth.

The End

Description of the scenes in Salzburg

Today, the city of Salzburg has approximately 144,000 inhabitants and is the fourth largest city in Austria. The word Salzburg means "Salt Castle". The name was derived from the city's salt mines and the fortress located in the center of town. The river Salzach divides the city into two parts – the left and right banks. In former times, the area of Salzburg was ruled by the church. Their rulers were called archbishops.

Leopoldskron Palace

Gaisberg Mountain

Front:

Leopoldskron Palace was built by Archbishop Leopold Anton Firmian. In the 20th century, it was the residence of the famous stage director Max Reinhardt, one of the founders of the Salzburg Festivals.

On the left side, you can see **Gaisberg Mountain.** This is the city's signature mountain, (height 1288m [4226 feet]) and it can easily be spotted by the broadcast transmitter at the top of it. It is an attractive destination for many hikers, bikers and nature lovers. In 1929, a road was built that has lead to the top of the mountain ever since. This road is quite popular with motorcyclists as well as convertible and antique car owners.

cathedral

Frohnburg Palace

Page 1:

The older part of "Old Town" is situated on the left bank of the river. The **cathedral** was built under the Archbishops Wolf Dietrich and Markus Sittikus. On the square in front of the cathedral, the play "Jedermann" [Everyman] by Hugo von Hofmannsthal is performed every summer. The **Hohensalzburg fortress** is the town's landmark and is situated on the Festungsberg [Fortress Mountain], 119 meters [390 feet] above the city. The fortress can be reached on foot or by special tram. The fortress is also famous for its "Salzburger Stier", a huge horn that was blown in former times when the town gates were opened each morning and closed every evening. Today, the horn sounds every morning at 11 o'clock in the summer. Keep this in mind the next time you happen to be standing in the cathedral square at this time of day.

On the right side, you can see the **Nonnberg Abbey** which was founded in 700 AD by holy Rupert for his niece Erentrudis. Today, it is the oldest remaining convent throughout the entire German speaking region.

Page 2:

Frohnburg Palace is situated in the middle of Hellbrunn Parkway and was built in 1672 as a simple country estate for an earl. In the film "The Sound of Music", the entrance of the palace served as the residence for the aristocratic family that Maria joined.

Page 3 top:

Imberg Street is on the right side of the Salzach River and consists of a long row of buildings with many historically significant houses. The Imberg staircase can be used to reach Capuchin Mountain [Kapuzinerberg], which offers a magnificent view of the city.

Hohensalzburg fortress

Nonnberg Abbey

Imbert Street

Mirabell stairs

Hellbrunn Palace

Monatsschlössl

Pavilion

Page 3 bottom:

In the Mirabell Palace, you can see the beautiful **marble staircase** which leads to the world famous **wedding salon.** The marble staircase is decorated with sculptures from Georg Raphael Donner. He created little round figures from stone (Untersberg marble) that frolic along the balustrade. Today, many concerts are held in the castle. In addition, the Mirabell Palace is home to the office of the mayor and the Salzburg city council.

Page 4:

The Hellbrunn Parkway (closed to automobiles) is an old path lined with trees and castles connecting the city and **Hellbrunn Palace.** The palace was built in 1613 AD under Archbishop Markus Sittikus and its architecture was inspired by the Italian school. The pleasure garden with its **trick fountains** is of particular interest to visitors. The **"Monatsschlössl"** Castle on the slope of the Hellbrunn Mountain is part of this area as well. According to legend, it was built in just a single month. Numerous visitors come to see the Hellbrunn Zoo and the **Stone Theatre,** the oldest open-air theatre north of the Alps, which was developed from the same quarry that was used to construct the Palace of Hellbrunn. In Hellbrunn Park, you will find the famous pavilion that appeared in the film "The Sound of Music".

The **Untersberg Mountain** rises majestically behind the area of Hellbrunn reaching a height of 1852m [6076 feet]. Proficient climbers can explore the mountain on foot; others are free to take a cable car. For many years, marble has been gathered from inside the mountain and is known throughout the world as Untersberg marble.

wedding salon

trick fountains

Stone Theatre

Untersberg Mountain

Felsenreitschule

Horsepond

Mirabell Garden

Fiaker

Page 8:
In former times, the town of Salzburg had feasts with public spectacles that sometimes lasted several days. The **"Felsenreitschule"** was built under Archbishop Wolf Dietrich. He also had the galleries in the stone walls of the "Mönchsberg" mountain engraved. The audience took their place in these galleries to admire the artistic feats of the elegant horses that trotted by. The Felsenreitschule has served as a performance area for the Salzburg Festivals since 1926.

Page 10:
The Horsepond was built by Michael Bernhard Mandl in 1695, approximately 50 years before Mozart was born. The **Horsepond** shows a variety of horse paintings that display the temperaments of various breeds of horses. The "Mönchsberg" mountain makes for a scenic backdrop to the Horsepond. This steep cliff wall must be inspected regularly for loose pieces of stone. Brave men conduct this work by maneuvering along the wall while attached to a rope and hammering against the mountain. These men are called "Berg-putzer" or "mountain fettlers".

Back:
The Mirabell Garden is a geometric park of remarkable beauty. It was designed by Fisher von Erlach. The garden's most notable attractions are the Pegasus fountain in the middle of the park as well as the rose hill, which offers a view of the castle, the city and a grassy area populated by a number of garden gnomes (made of marble from Untersberg Mountain).

In the city, you will encounter quite a few horse-drawn carriages called "Fiaker". These carriages are also allowed to enter the pedestrian zone. Most agree that these carriages suit the atmosphere of the city.

Gnomes

About the author:
Margret Springl was born in 1969 in Kuchl near Salzburg, Austria.
After graduating, she travelled to the US to spend time there.

The book The Singing Family from Salzburg was created under her artful instruction.

About the illustrator:
Regine Otrel was born in 1940 in Dresden, Germany.
She has lived in Mondsee near Salzburg for many years.

She currently teaches painting and drawing to children.

Contact:

Margret Springl
E-Mail: ms.office@aon.at
www.salzburgbook.com

Impressum:

Pictures: Tourismus Salzburg GmbH, Davide Mauri
Historical contribution: Mag. Christiana Schneeweiss · www.kultur-tourismus.com
Scenes of illustrations: Matis family (Nicholas, Ilse, Viktoria, Johanna)
Proofreading: MB Sprach-Übersetzungsbüro · www.boensch.at
Features: POLAK and friends GmbH, Werbeagentur · www.32.polakandfriends.com
Setting: Media Design Rizner

Many thanks to all, not personally mentioned ones.